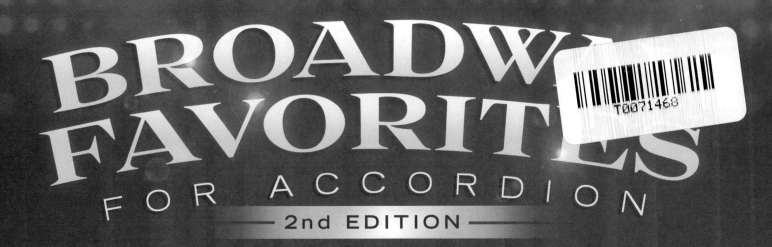

BROADWAY FAVORITES
FOR ACCORDION
— 2nd EDITION —

ISBN 978-1-4950-8468-3

HAL•LEONARD®

7777 W. BLUEMOUND RD. P.O. BOX 13819 MILWAUKEE, WI 53213

Visit Hal Leonard Online at
www.halleonard.com

CLIMB EV'RY MOUNTAIN
from THE SOUND OF MUSIC

Lyrics by OSCAR HAMMERSTEIN II
Music by RICHARD RODGERS

With deep feeling

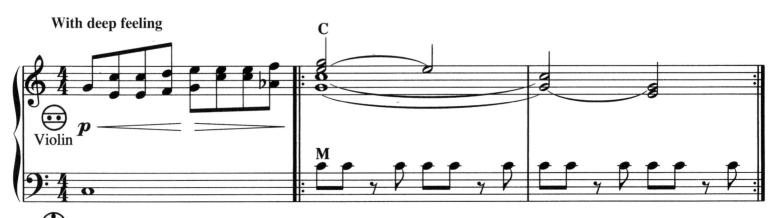

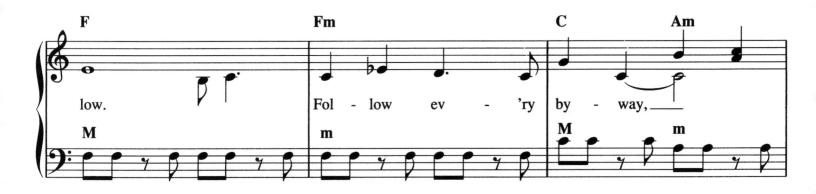

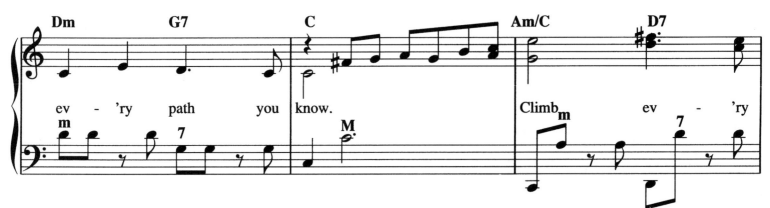

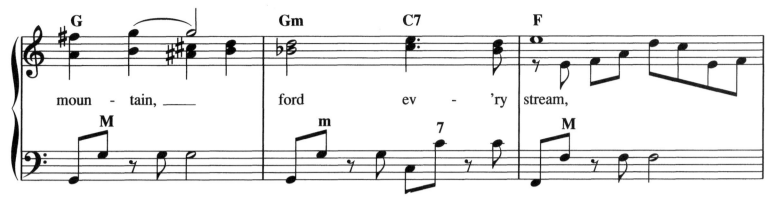

mountain, ____ ford ev - 'ry stream,

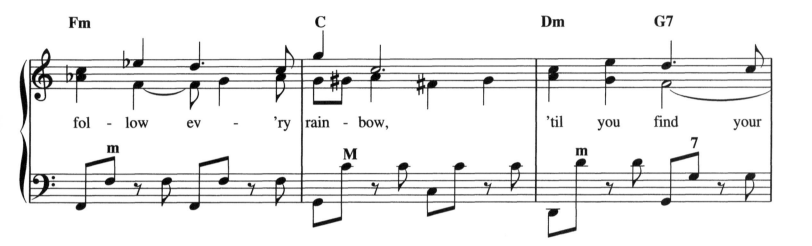

fol - low ev - 'ry rain - bow, 'til you find your

dream! A dream that will need____ all the love you can give,____

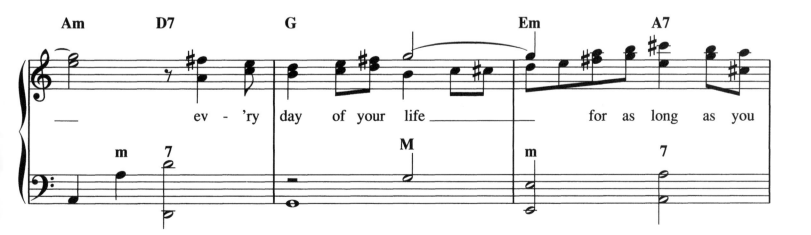

____ ev - 'ry day of your life ____ for as long as you

4

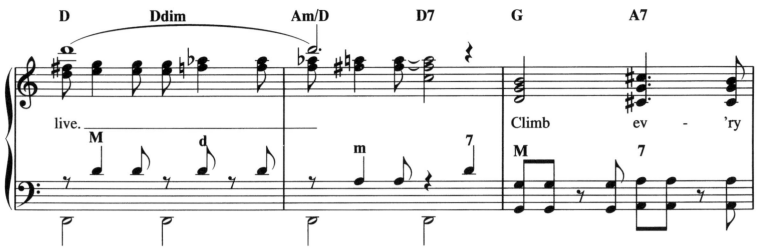

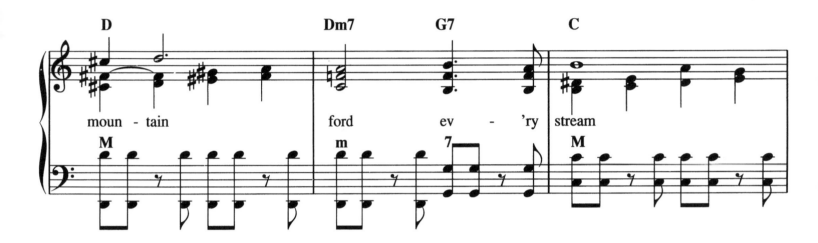

DON'T CRY FOR ME ARGENTINA

from EVITA

Words by TIM RICE
Music by ANDREW LLOYD WEBBER

Slow Latin feel

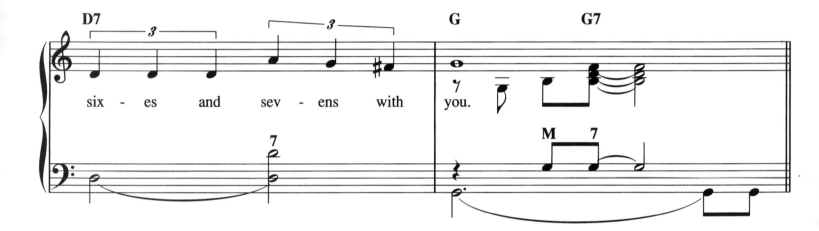

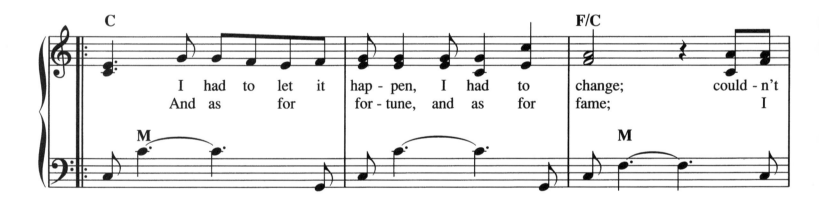

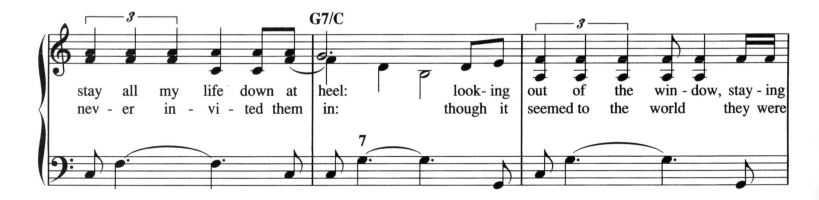

out of the sun. _____ So I choose free - dom
all I de - sired. _____ They are il - lu - sions they're

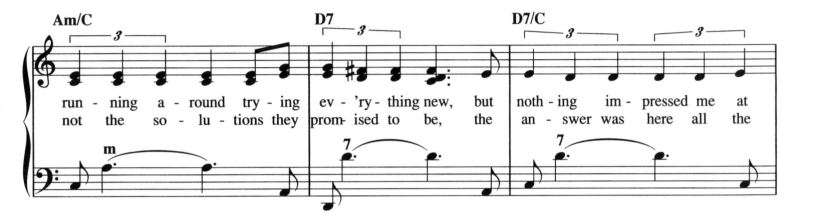

run - ning a - round try - ing ev - 'ry - thing new, but noth - ing im - pressed me at
not the so - lu - tions they prom - ised to be, the an - swer was here all the

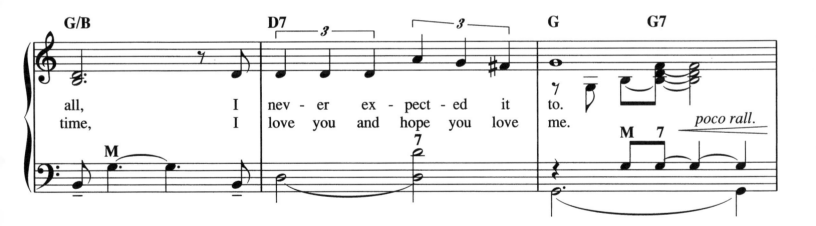

all, I nev - er ex - pect - ed it to.
time, I love you and hope you love me.

Don't cry for me Ar - gen - ti - na _____ the truth is I nev - er

left you. ____ All through my | wild days, ____ my mad ex - | ist - ence, ____ I kept my

prom - ise, ____ don't keep your | dis - tance. ____ |

Have I said too much? There's | noth - ing more I can think of to | say to you,

but | all you have to do is

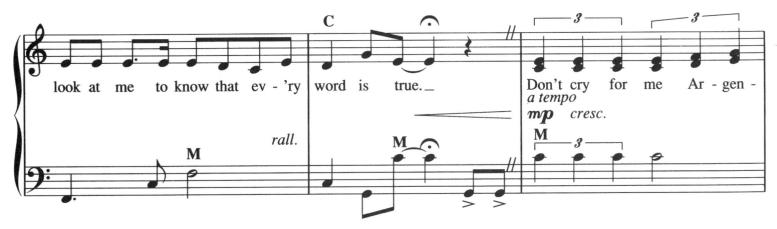

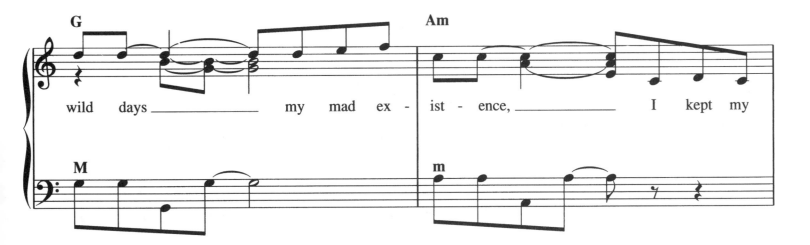

EDELWEISS

from THE SOUND OF MUSIC

Lyrics by OSCAR HAMMERSTEIN II
Music by RICHARD RODGERS

Slowly, with expression

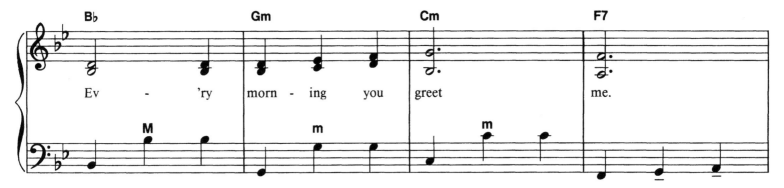

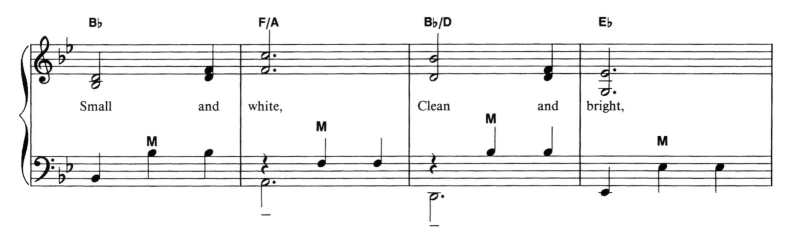

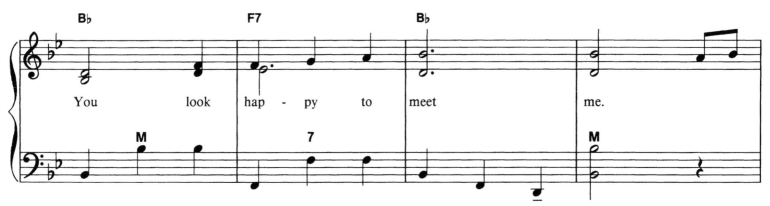

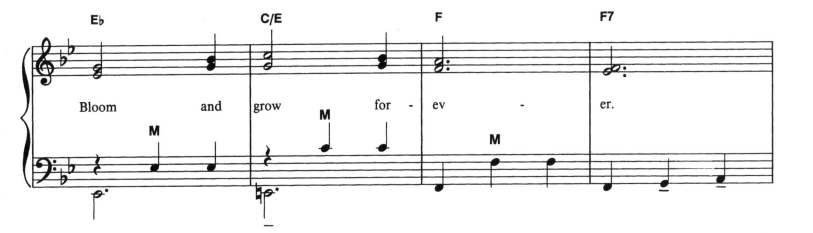

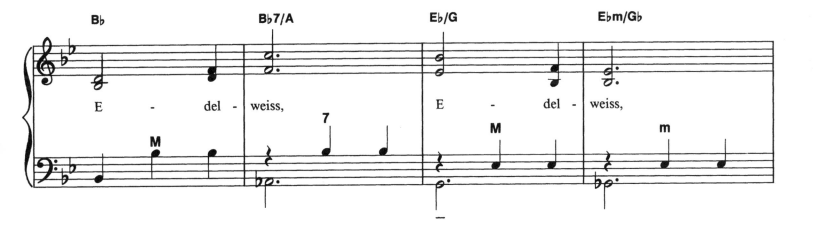

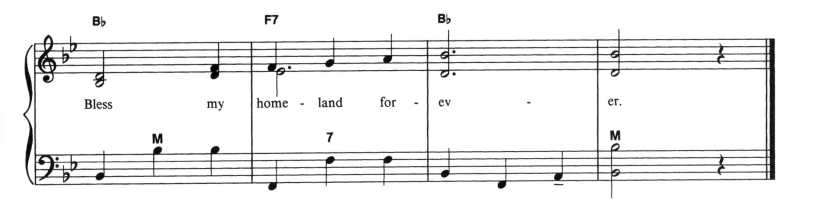

I GOT RHYTHM

from AN AMERICAN IN PARIS
from GIRL CRAZY

Music and Lyrics by GEORGE GERSHWIN
and IRA GERSHWIN

I _____ got rhy - thm, _____
I _____ got dais - ies _____

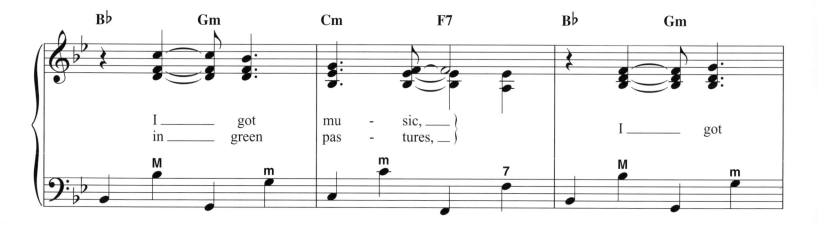

I _____ got mu - sic, _____
in _____ green pas - tures, _____

I _____ got

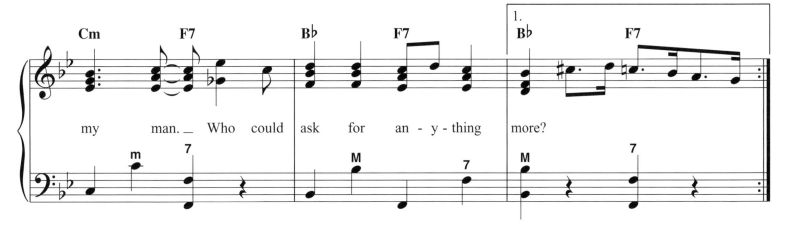

my man.___ Who could ask for an - y - thing more?

more? Old ____ Man Trou - ble, ___

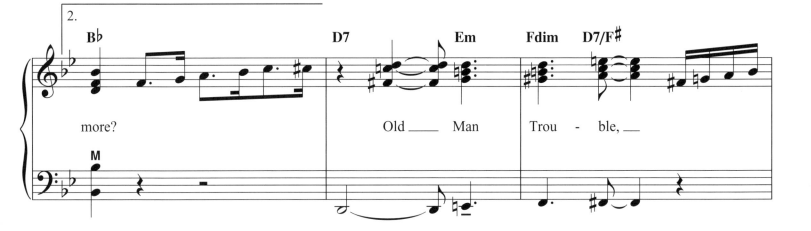

I _____ don't mind him. ___ You ___ won't

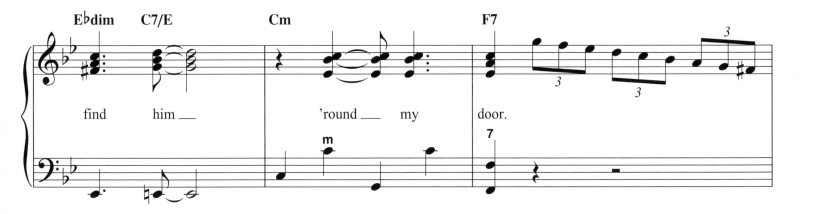

find him ___ 'round ___ my door.

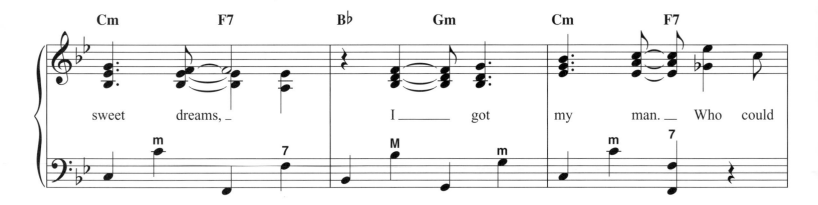

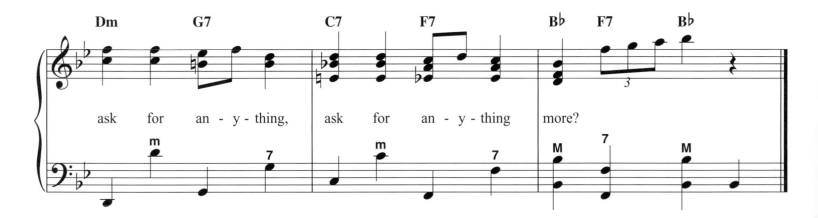

GETTING TO KNOW YOU
from THE KING AND I

Lyrics by OSCAR HAMMERSTEIN II
Music by RICHARD RODGERS

Gracefully; not too fast

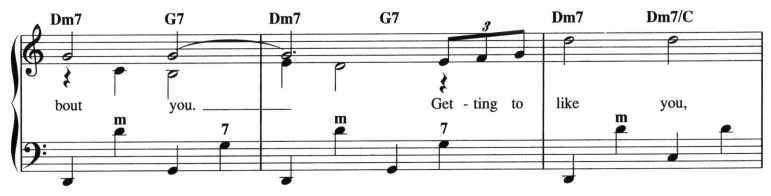

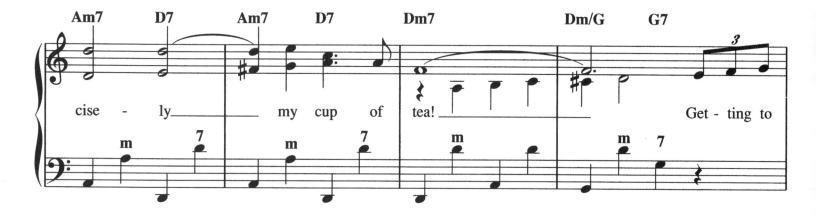

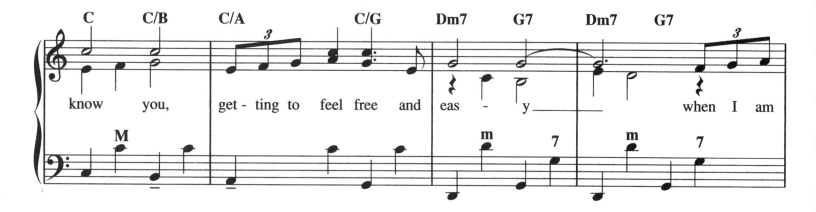

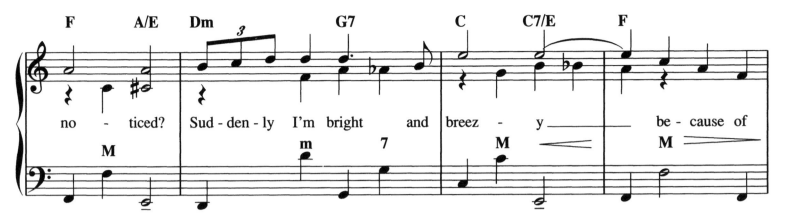

no - ticed? Sud - den - ly I'm bright and breez - y _____ be - cause of

all the beau - ti - ful and new things I'm learn - ing a - bout you

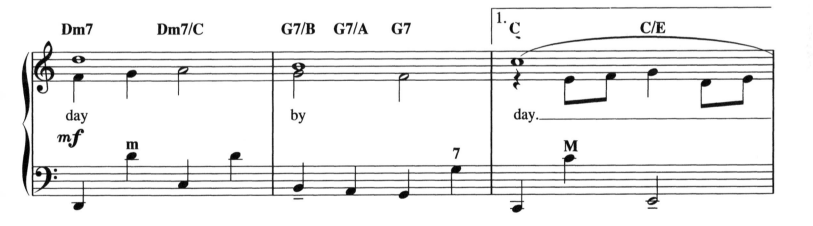

day by day.

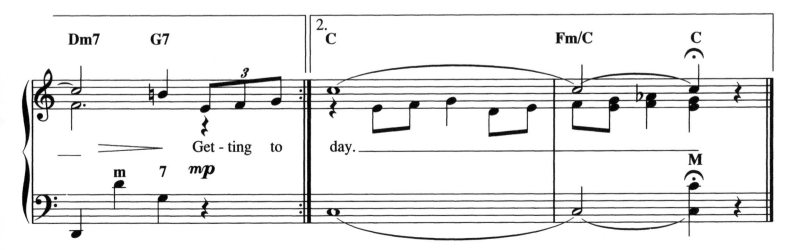

Get - ting to day.

I WHISTLE A HAPPY TUNE

from THE KING AND I

Lyrics by OSCAR HAMMERSTEIN II
Music by RICHARD RODGERS

strike a care-less pose and whis-tle a hap-py tune and

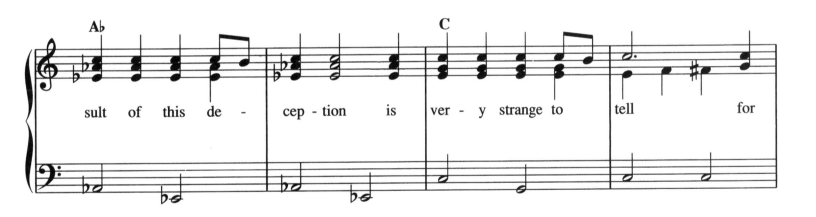

no one ev-er knows I'm a-fraid ___ The re-

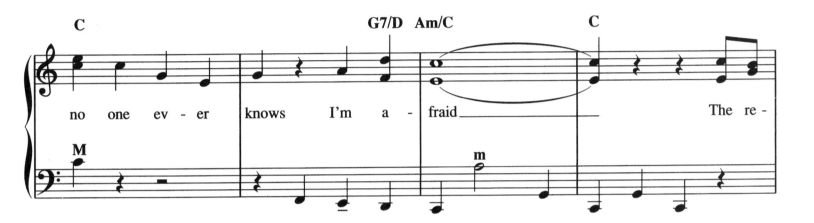

sult of this de-cep-tion is ver-y strange to tell for

when I fool the peo-ple I fear I fool my-self as well! I

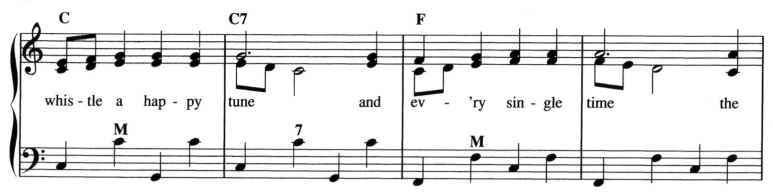

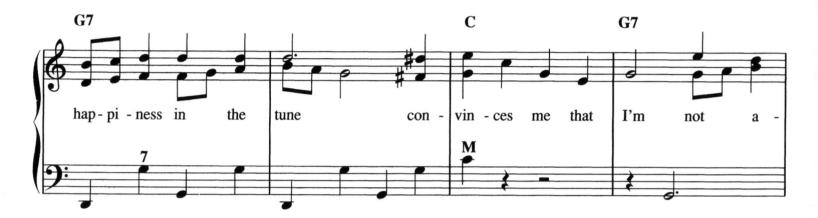

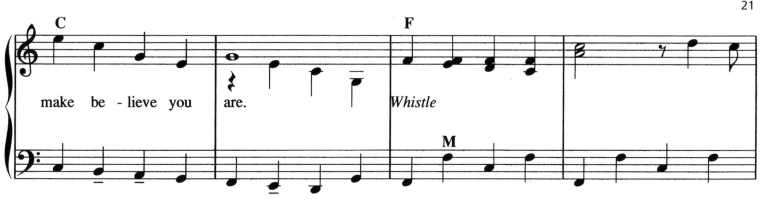

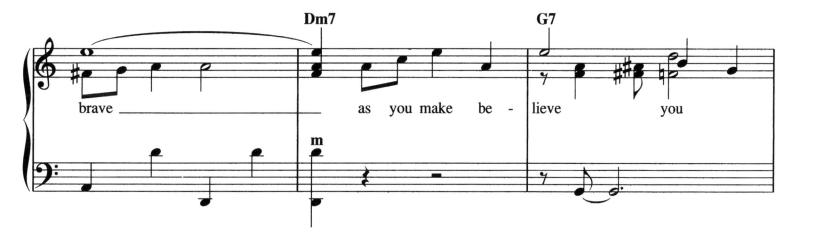

IF I WERE A RICH MAN

from the Musical FIDDLER ON THE ROOF

Words by SHELDON HARNICK
Music by JERRY BOCK

Lilting

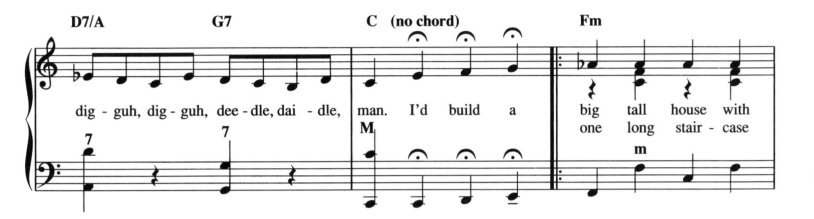

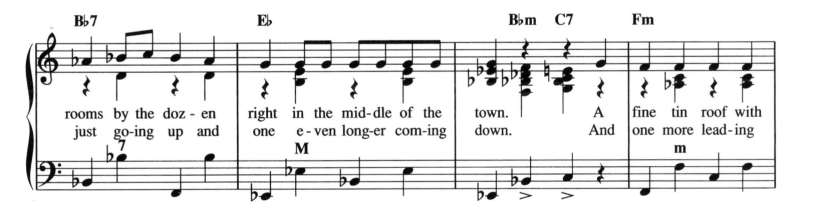

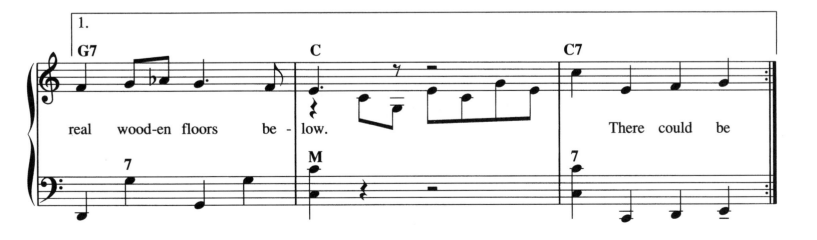

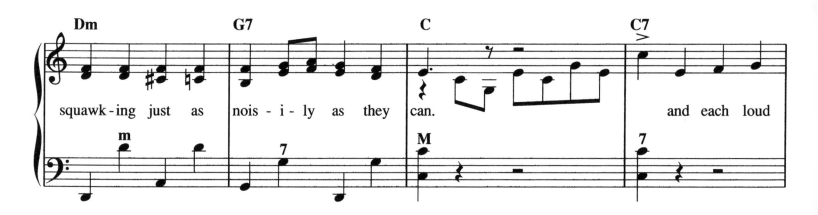

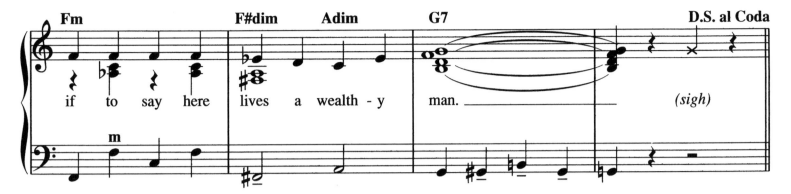

Fm   F#dim   Adim   G7   **D.S. al Coda**

if to say here lives a wealth - y man. _____ *(sigh)*

CODA

G7   Cm   G7

Lord, who made the   li - on and the lamb.   You de - creed I

rubato

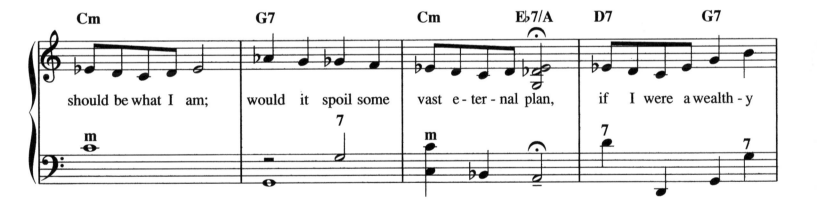

Cm   G7   Cm   E♭7/A   D7   G7

should be what I am;   would it spoil some   vast e - ter - nal plan,   if I were a wealth - y

C   **no chord**   G7   C

man. _____

a tempo

IT MIGHT AS WELL BE SPRING

from STATE FAIR

Lyrics by OSCAR HAMMERSTEIN II
Music by RICHARD RODGERS

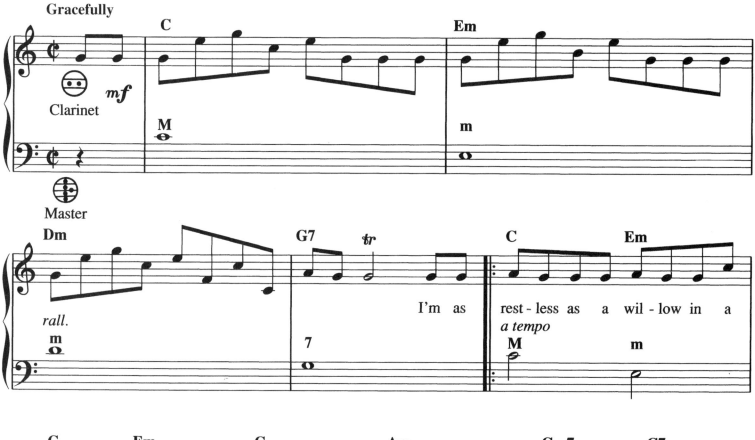

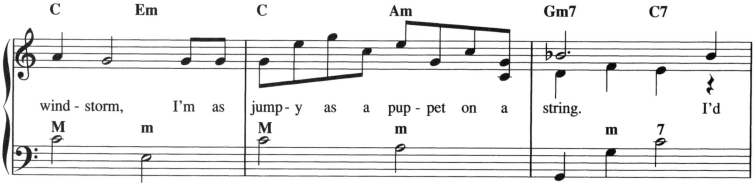

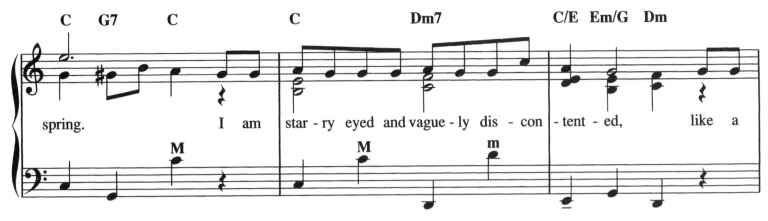

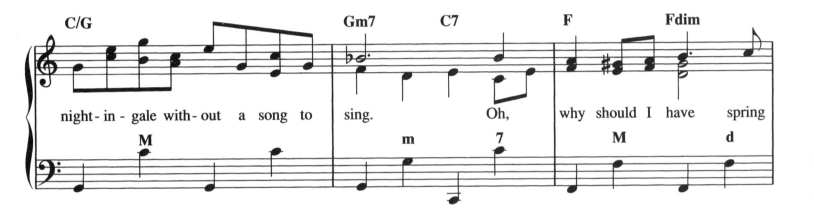

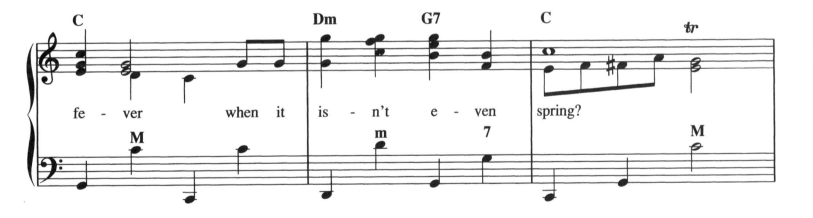

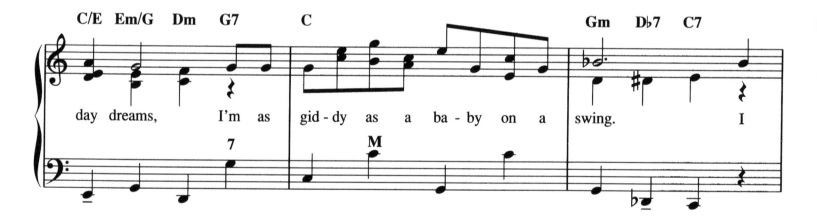

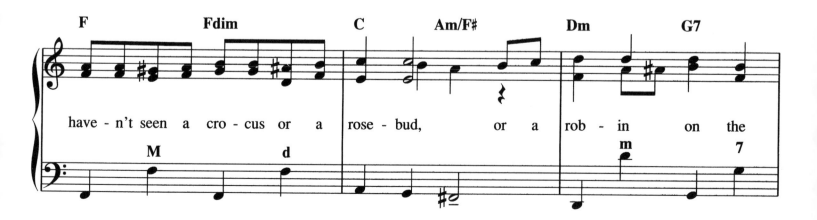

THE LONELY GOATHERD
from THE SOUND OF MUSIC

Lyrics by OSCAR HAMMERSTEIN II
Music by RICHARD RODGERS

Brightly, with a lilt

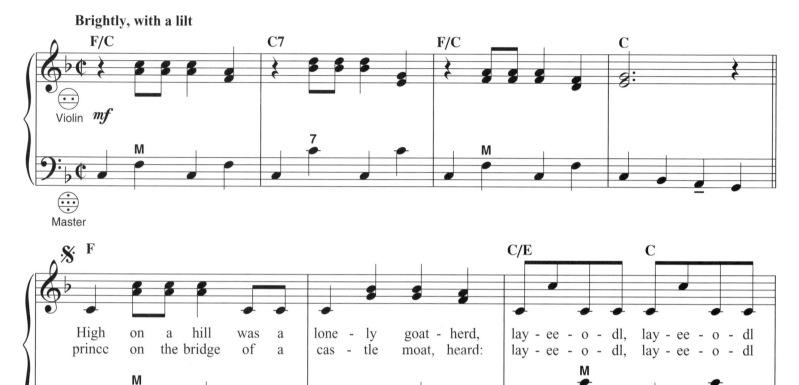

High on a hill was a lone-ly goat-herd, lay-ee-o-dl, lay-ee-o-dl
prince on the bridge of a cas-tle moat, heard: lay-ee-o-dl, lay-ee-o-dl

lay-ee-o. Loud was the voice of the lone-ly goat-herd,
lay-ee-o. Men on a road, with a load to tote, heard:

lay-ee-o-dl, lay-ee-o-dl-o. Folks in a town that was
lay-ee-o-dl, lay-ee-o-dl-o. Men in the midst of a

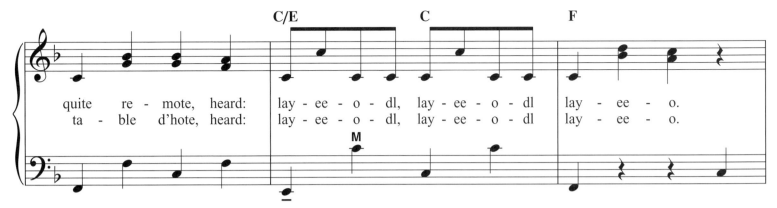

quite re - mote, heard: lay - ee - o - dl, lay - ee - o - dl lay - ee - o.
ta - ble d'hote, heard: lay - ee - o - dl, lay - ee - o - dl lay - ee - o.

Lust - y and clear from the goat - herd's throat, heard: lay - ee - o - dl, lay - ee - o - dl -
Men drink - ing beer with the foam a - float, heard: lay - ee - o - dl, lay - ee - o - dl -

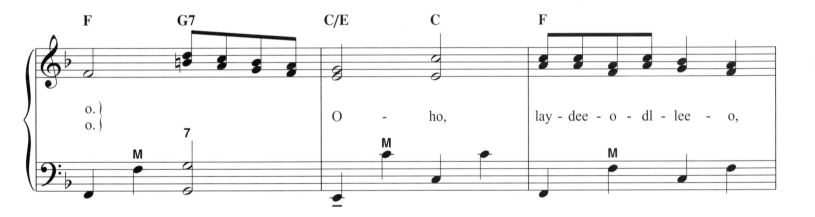

o.
o.
O - ho, lay - dee - o - dl - lee - o,

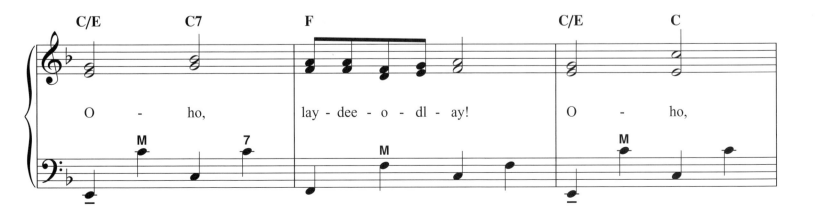

O - ho, lay - dee - o - dl - ay! O - ho,

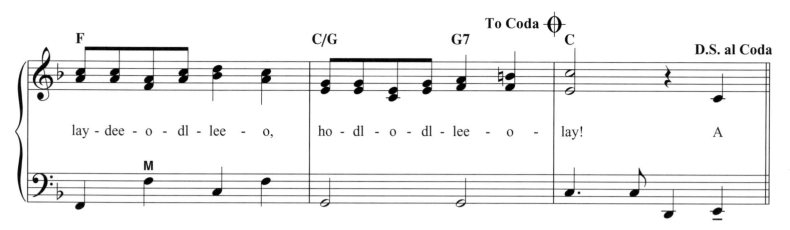

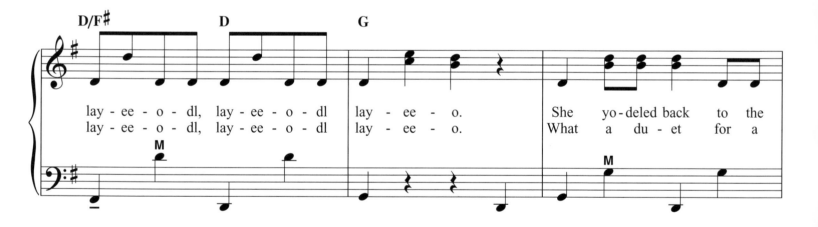

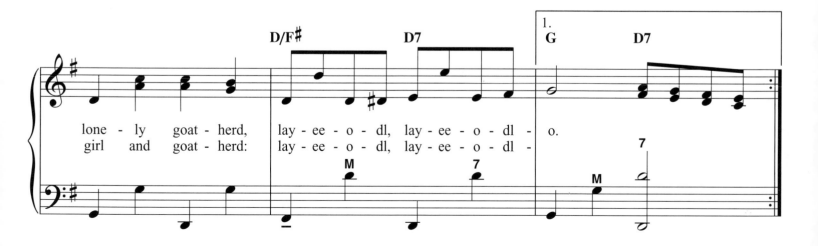

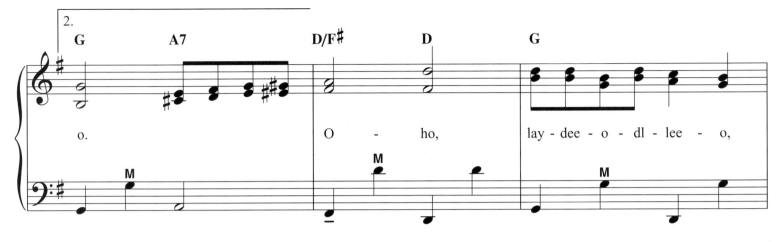

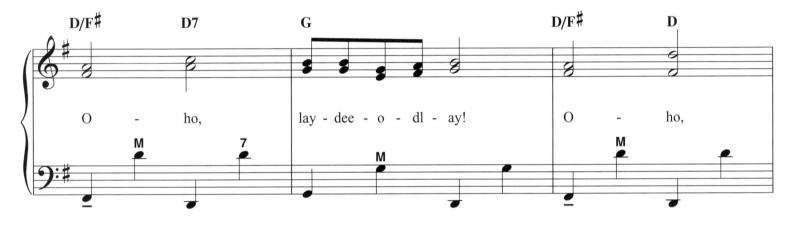

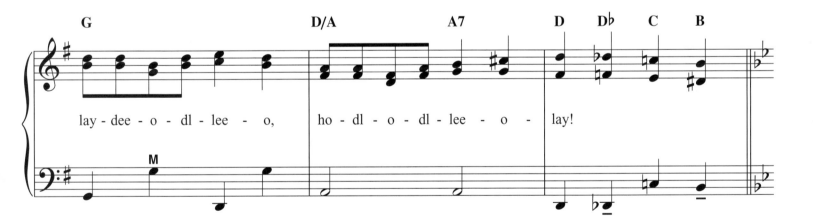

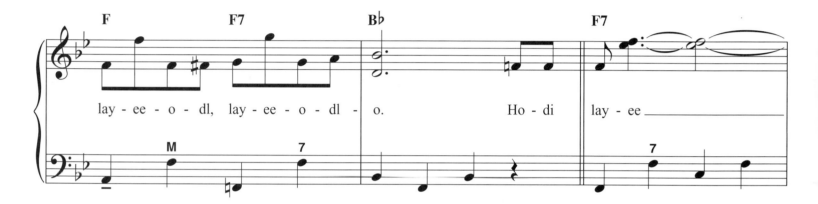

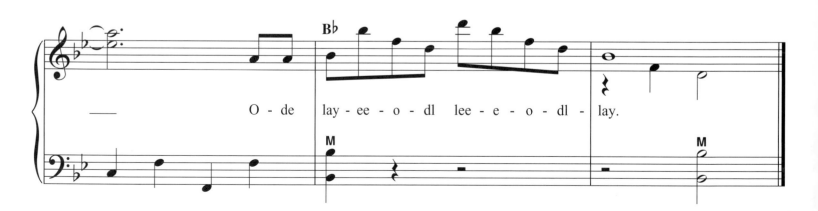

OH, WHAT A BEAUTIFUL MORNIN'
from OKLAHOMA

Lyrics by OSCAR HAMMERSTEIN II
Music by RICHARD RODGERS

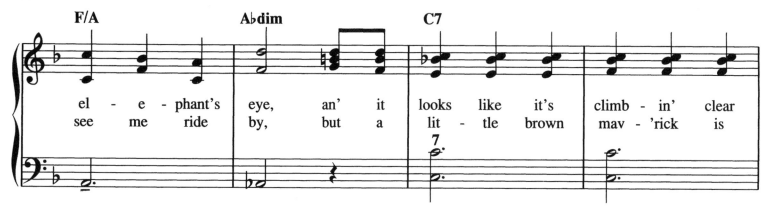

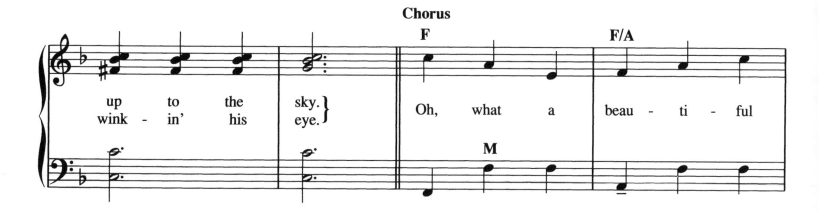

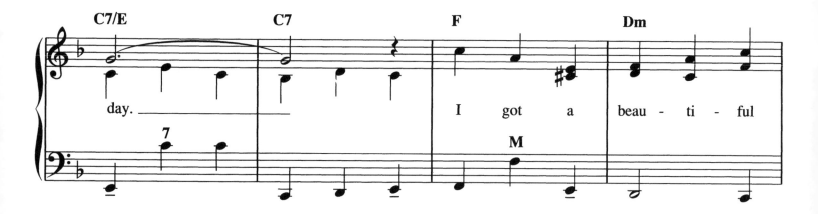

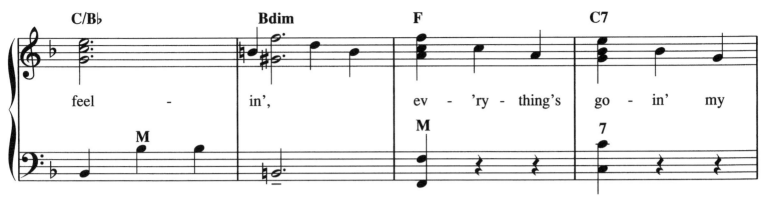

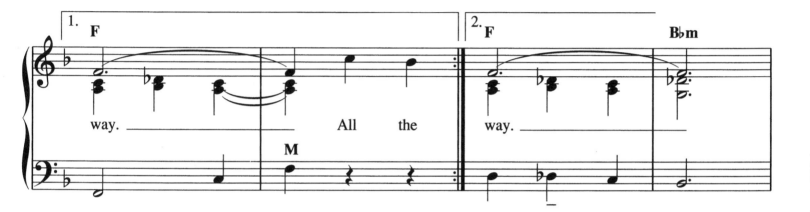

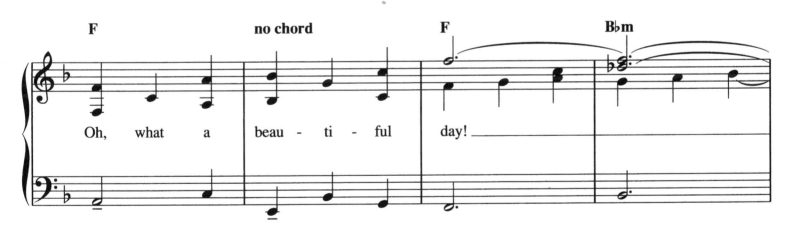

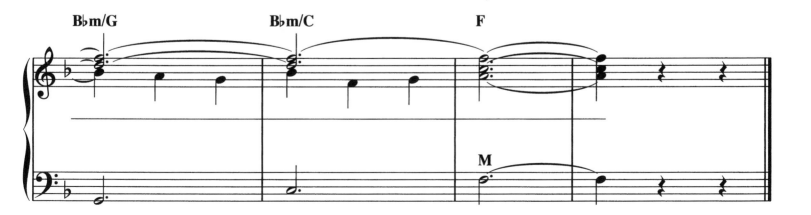

MATCHMAKER
from the Musical FIDDLER ON THE ROOF

Words by SHELDON HARNICK
Music by JERRY BOCK

Tempo di Valse

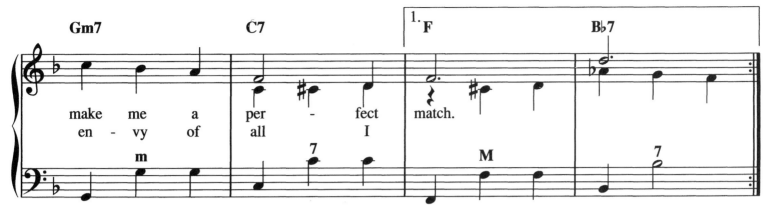

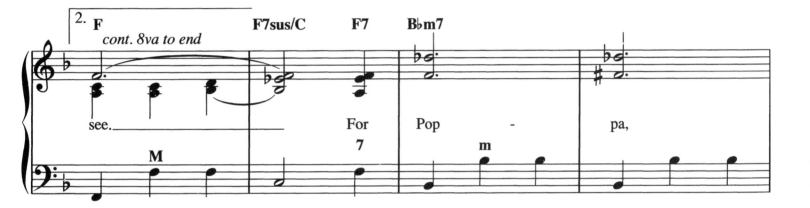

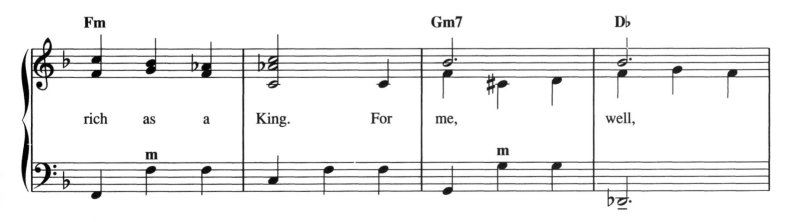

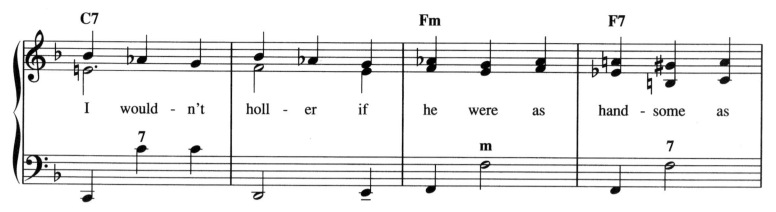

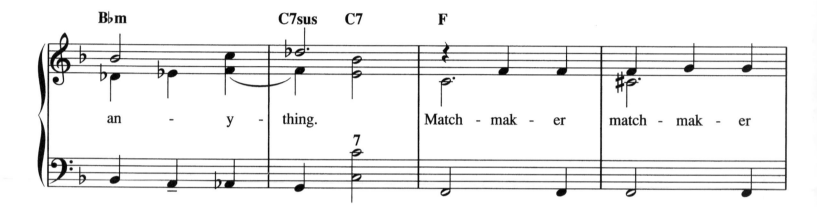

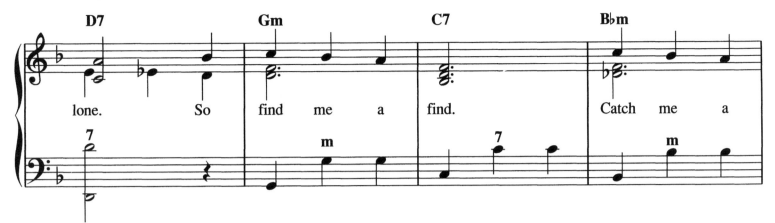

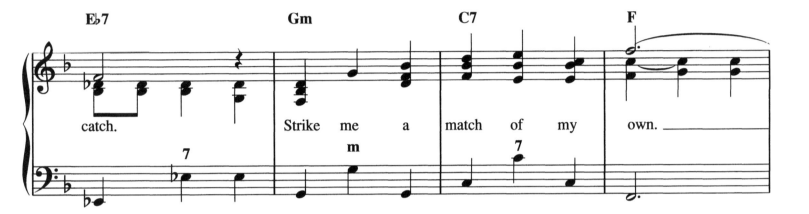

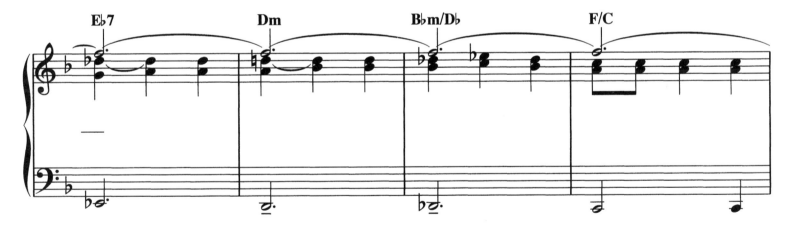

SUNRISE, SUNSET
from the Musical FIDDLER ON THE ROOF

Words by SHELDON HARNICK
Music by JERRY BOCK

Moderately slow Waltz tempo

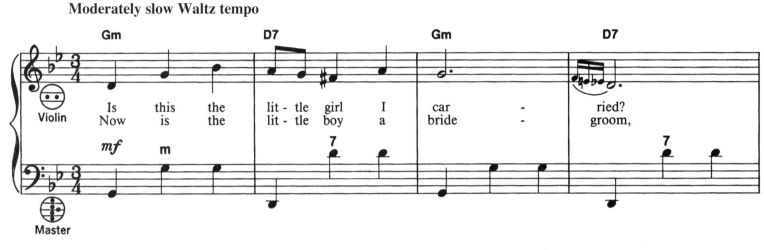

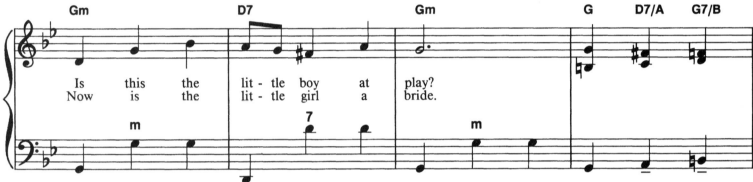

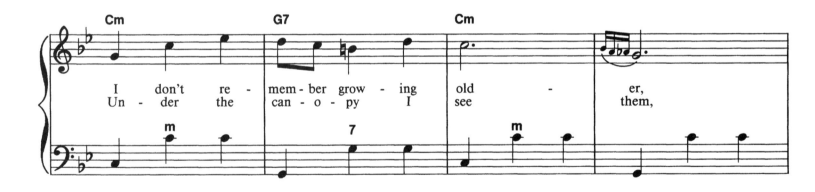

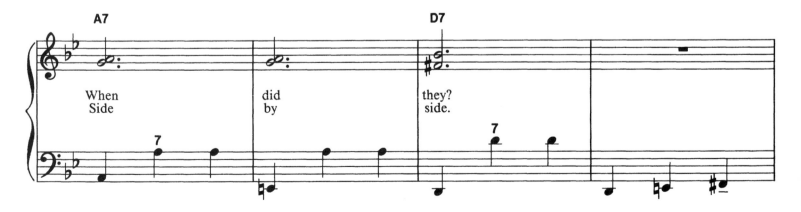

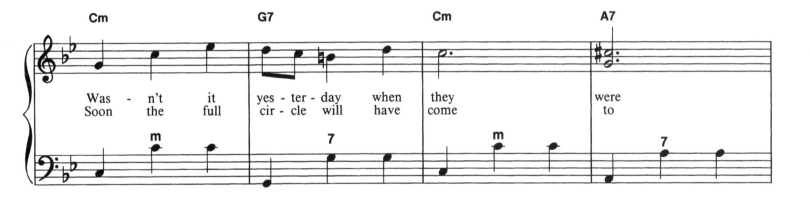

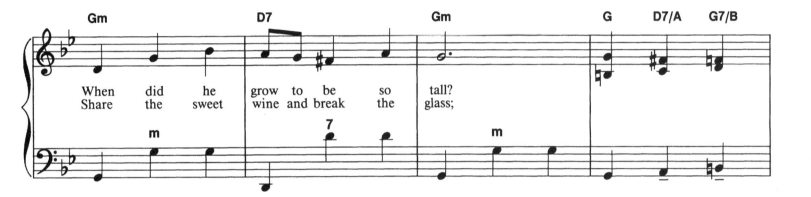

44

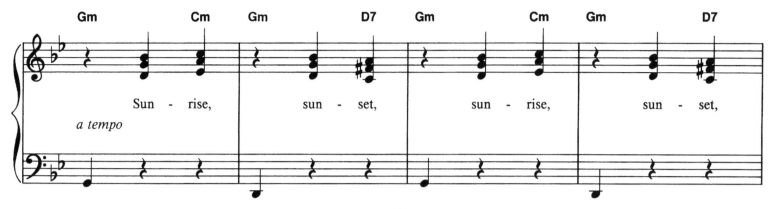

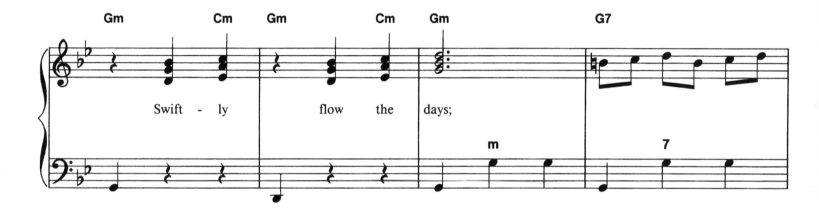

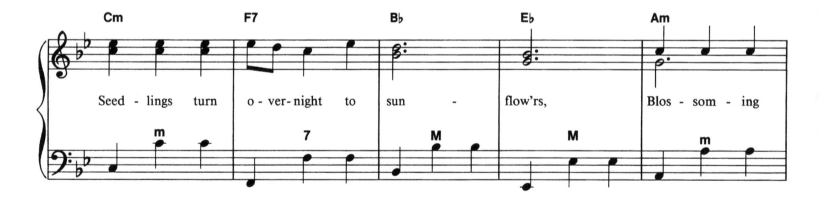

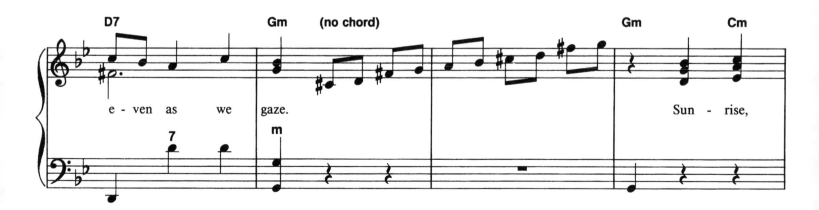

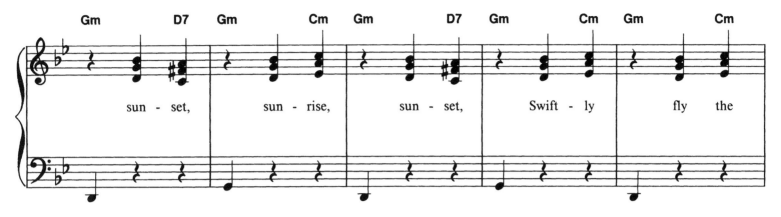

sun - set, sun - rise, sun - set, Swift - ly fly the

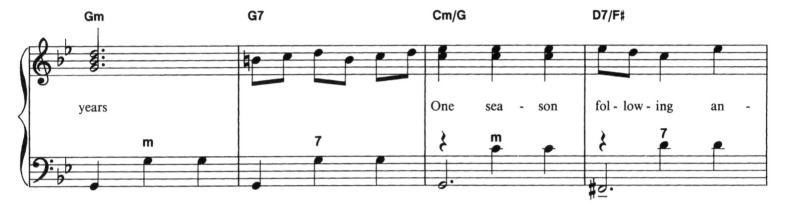

years One sea - son fol - low - ing an -

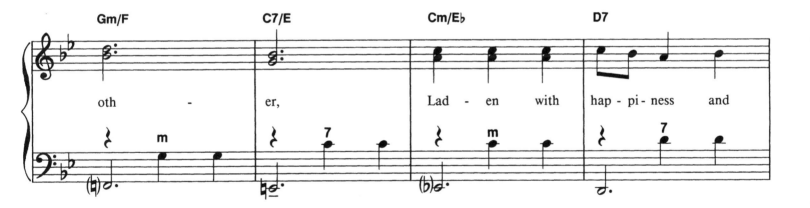

oth - er, Lad - en with hap - pi - ness and

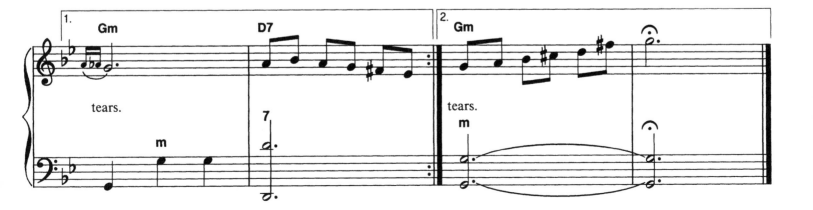

tears. tears.

WHATEVER LOLA WANTS
(Lola Gets)
from DAMN YANKEES

Words and Music by RICHARD ADLER
and JERRY ROSS

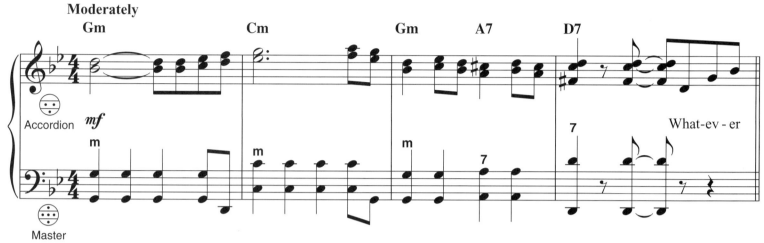

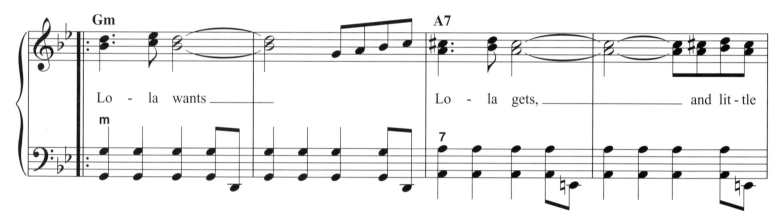

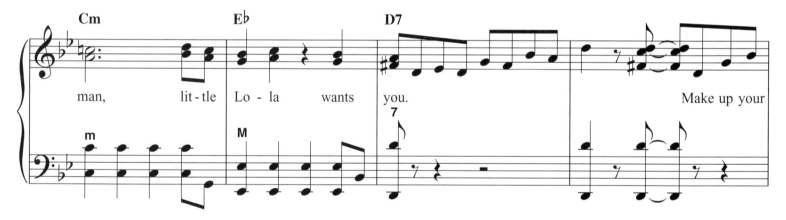

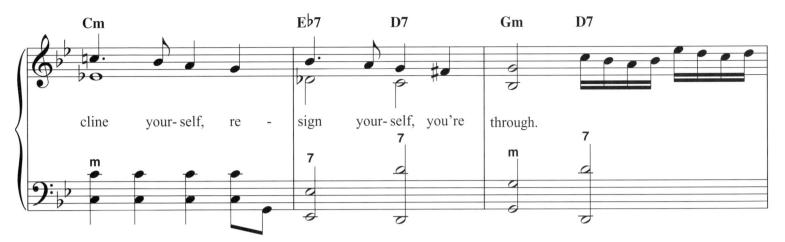

cline your-self, re - sign your-self, you're through.

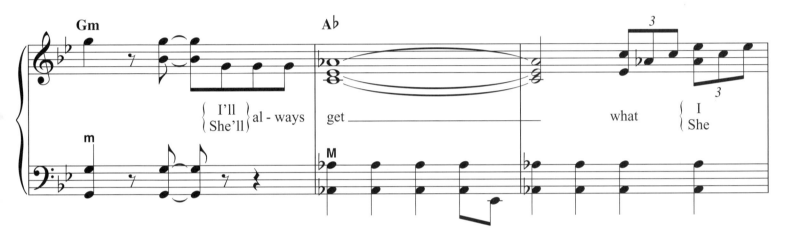

I'll She'll al - ways get _____ what I She

aim aims for. _____ And your heart and soul

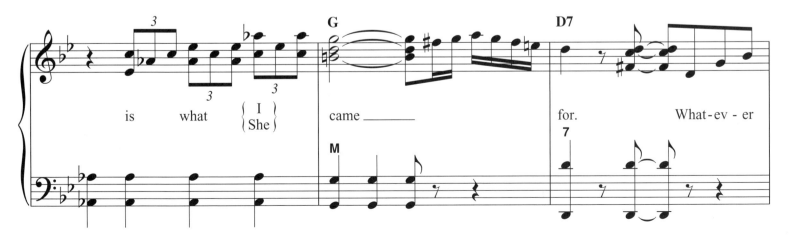

is what I She came _____ for. What-ev - er

Lo - la wants ____ Lo - la gets, ____ take off your

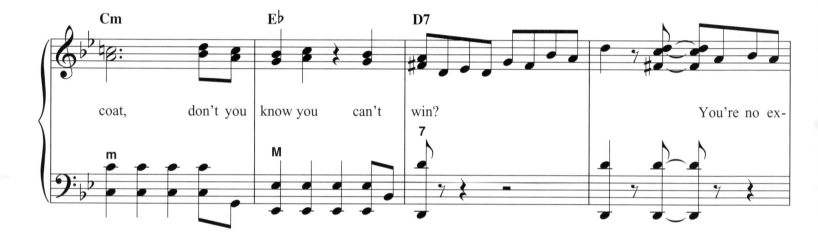

coat, don't you know you can't win? You're no ex-

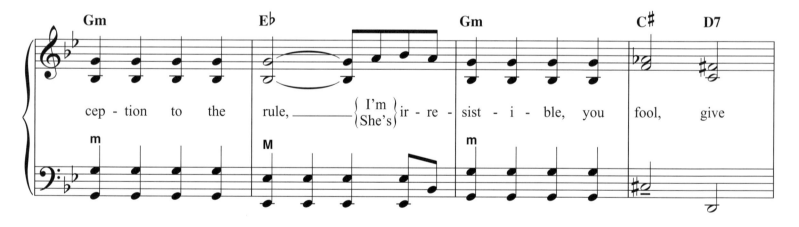

cep - tion to the rule, ____ {I'm / She's} ir - re - sist - i - ble, you fool, give

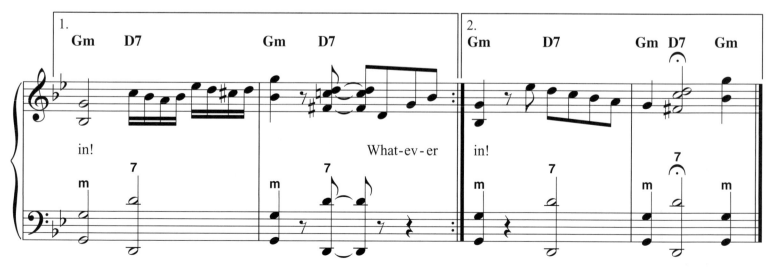

1.
in! What-ev - er in!

2.
in!